TROGIR

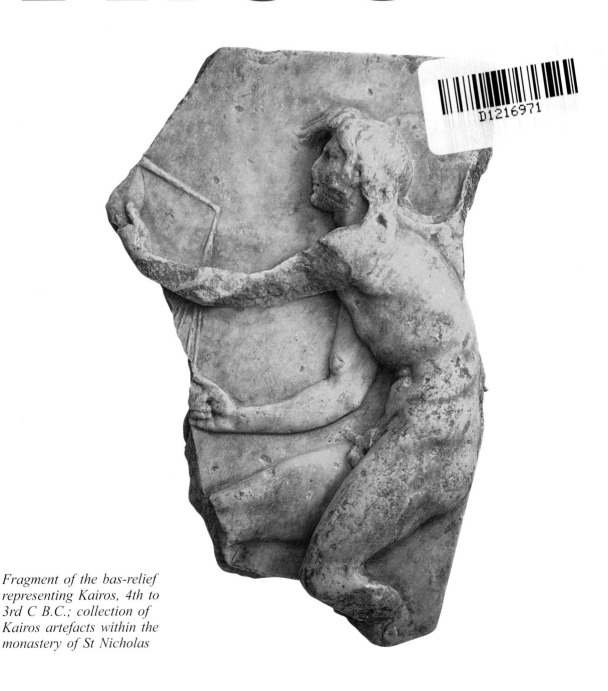

Fragment of the bas-relief representing Kairos, 4th to 3rd C B.C.; collection of Kairos artefacts within the monastery of St Nicholas

Series

HERITAGE

No 1

ISBN 953-215-267-9

Editors

Ana Ivelja-Dalmatin

Davor Nikolić

Mato Njavro

Marija Vranješ

Milan Vukelić

Editor-in-Chief

Mato Njavro

Responsible editor

Ana Ivelja-Dalmatin

Art editor

Milan Vukelić

Publisher

TN Turistička naklada d.o.o., Zagreb

For publisher

Marija Vranješ

Photolithographs

O-TISAK, Zagreb

Print

Vjesnik d.d., Zagreb

TROGIR

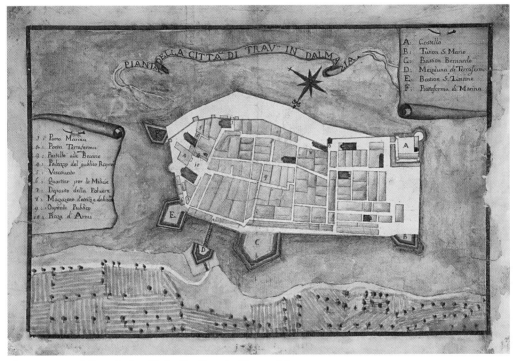

Layout of Trogir, middle of the 18th C., Trogir Town Museum

Text
FANI CELIO CEGA

Translated by
Margareta Deletis Novaković

Photos
Milan Babić, Živko Bačić, Andrija Carli, Branko Ostojić, Ivo Pervan

Zagreb, 2006.

Trogir ⇨

TOWN WHICH HAS EXISTED FROM ANCIENT TIMES

The curving grid of Trogir's streets, adorned with Romanesque, Gothic and Renaissance facades, characterizes its architectural rhythm of picturesque stone, rhythm that flows through its buildings, enters its court yards, touches its tile roofs, flourishes on its windows, enters through balconies and church steeples...

(Cvito Fisković)

The main factors that contributed to the founding of Trogir were its natural sheltered position, wide bay, convenient location on an islet between the shore and the island of Čiovo, mild winters, and a strategically important location. Many different peoples lived in this small area, assimilating with each other: the Illyrians, Greeks, Romans and Croatians. The area was ruled by the Venetians, Franks (French) and Austrians. All of them left imprints on the town, but most importantly the Croatians who, together with their language, managed to survive the turbulent centuries of Trogir's history.

Present day Trogir with approximately 13,000 inhabitants is located in the Splitsko-Dalmatinska county on the western side of the Kaštelanski bay. It is close to the Jadranska Highway and is well connected with other towns and cities in its vicinity, such as Kaštela, Solin, and Split. It also has convenient links with the surrounding boroughs of Segeta, Marina and Okrug (on the island of Čiovo) which used to be under its auspices. Frequent bus routes to the surrounding areas and other large Croatian cities make it an easily accessible destination. It has good ferry connections (more frequent during the summer season) with Split as well as the neighboring islands of Drvenik Veliki and Drvenik Mali. The proximity of the international airport contributes to it being well connected with the rest of the world.

Trogir has an indented coastline consisting of many bays, capes, and islands flourishing with Mediterranean plants. Most of these are completely preserved in their natural beauty and are therefore attractive to those who enjoy sailing along the Adriatic coast. Trogir has a pleasant climate with mild winters and warm summers, that are cooled by a gentle wind called maestral.

Trogir's turbulent history and legacy of its stone structures contributed to it becoming one of the UNESCO's World Heritage sites.

⇦ *Trogir bell-towers*

Trogir quay ⇨

HISTORICAL BACKGROUND

Antiquity

The settlement of Trogir was established at the end of the third or the beginning of second century BC. The Greeks, Dorans from Syracuse, and merchants of the Antiquity Issa established a merchant colony on the peninsula and named it Tragurion. It is speculated that the name comes from the Greek words tragos and oros (goat and hill), which lead to the conclusion that Trogir could have gotten its name from the neighboring hill, frequented by herds of sheep, named Kozjak (*koza* means sheep in Croatian). Archeological excavations show that life in this area began in the early history. Burial mounds and caves dating to the prehistoric period have been found around the city, on the coast, and the island of Čiovo. Due to the constant rising of the sea, it has been impossible for the archeological diggings to reach the so called sterile level. Therefore it has not been proven when exactly life began in the Trogir area.

The oldest remains, buried below the present-day street level, are undergoing archeological excavations that will eventually complete the floor plan of the Antiquity Trogir. It is a know fact that present day layout of Trogir dates back the Greek times. During this period, the eastern part of the island was surrounded by dry wall. The present day city square is in the same location as it predecessor, a much narrower Ancient Greek square (*agora*). The layout of the surrounding streets resembles that of the Greek times.

During the civil war between Pompeii and Caesar that erupted in 49 BC, Trogir, allying itself with Pompeii, ended up on the losing side. The Greek colony established in this location in the first century BC became a municipality of the Roman Empire – the Roman Tragurium. The city necropolis was then located on the mainland, near the Dobrić well which was for a long time the main source of town's drinking water. In the beginning of the first century AD Emperor Claudius settled its retired veterans in the city's vicinity, in the settlement known as Sicula. The Roman oppidum was harvesting quality stone

Bas-relief representing a working woman, 2nd to 1st C B.C., Trogir Town Museum, stone collection ("lapidarij")

⇦ Northern town gate, 18th C

Courtyard of the Garagnin-Fanfogna Palace, Trogir Town Museum

from the stone pit located near a hill on which nowadays stands the renovated chapel of St. Ilija. Pleny the Elder (Naturalis Historia, III, 141) wrote about the Trogir stone pit in his Tragurium marmore civicum romanorum notum. Stone was harvested at this location during the Middle Ages, and the activity continued to this day at a near by site. A famous Peuntingerius' map from the Roman period includes the Trogir port, which points to its importance in those days. Very few material remains of the early Trogir history have been preserved. Some of them include: a relief of Kairos' face from the fourth or third century BC which can be found in the St. Nicholas monastery (samostan Sv. Nikole); a relief of a spinning woman's figure dating to the second or first century BC, located in the lapidary of the Museum of the town of Trogir (Muzej grada Trogira); terracotta arica with a bust of Hera belonging to a private collection; and a statue of Dionisius – Bakha from the first century AD, exhibited in the Archeological Museum of Split (Arheološki muzej u Splitu).

Early Christian Period

Christianity as a new religion spread to this city during the fourth century, in the period of late Antiquity. It most likely came from the

Stone collection in Trogir Town Museum

neighboring Salona, a place where the cult of Salona bishop and martyr, St. Dujmo, originated. The first Christian martyrs, according to a legend, gathered in a house in the vicinity of the Southern town gate. The gate was later referred to as Porta Domenica. The Preromanesque church of St. Dujmo was built in its location, while remains of an earlier, most likely early Christian, church were found underneath it. According to some stories, during the time of Constantine the Great, Christians built a basilica in Trogir. In the early fourth century the basilica dedicated to St. Lovro was renovated by a citizen of Solin, Quirinus. Archeological excavations on Travarica (near the present day fish market) where watering place for animals used to be, discovered remains of an early Christian basilica. During this time Trogir did not have a bishopric, but was under the jurisdiction of the Salona bishop. The first recorded bishop of Trogir was a certain Peter in the year of 700. Most of the early Christian remains, except for those built into the walls of churches and houses, can be found in the lapidary of the Museum of the Town of Trogir. Fourth century lead tablet, *Tabella plumbea Traguriensis*, is exceptionally interesting. It belongs to the so called tablets for the protection from curse, which were believed to magically scare away evil spirits. The tablet is

Altar pluteus with the cross ornament from the church of St Mary, 9th C A.D, Trogir Town Museum - "lapidarij"

In the middle of the sixth century, after years of fighting wars with the Goths, Dalmatia became a province. It was made into a **temat** of the Eastern Roman Empire, to be ruled and governed by the Byzantine Emperor and his Egzarhe in Ravena.

Together with the rest of the Dalmatian cities, Trogir was conquered by the Frank ruler Carl the Great during his war campaign from 804 to 805. His rule lasted until 814.

In his renowned work *De administrando imperio* (chapter 29) Byzantine Emperor and historian Constantine the Seventh Porfirogenet (10th century) vividly describes Trogir.

Two plaques from the eight and ninth century are a testimony to this period. The first one mentions Emperor Constantine (IN CONST [antinum] … [i]MPERATOREM). The second refers to the Emperor's member of staff, the Byzantine **themat** (Archeological Museum of Split). The presence of gold coins in the vicinity of the city is the evidence of the Frank rule. These coins bearing the name of Carl the Great were **solidus** of the Benevetian duke Gromolado the Third.

Governance by the Croatian National Rulers

From the seventh century on, the area was populated by new inhabitants, the Croats, who turned a new leaf of its history. Trogir is one of a few Dalmatian cities that was spared from destruction during this period of migration. The new population favored the city's sheltered position, and with their arrival the life in the city was forever changed. The name of Trogir remained until today. One of residencies of the Croatian rulers was in Bijaći and consisted of commercial buildings and living quarters. The oldest Croatian foundation of St. Martha (Sv. Marta) was also established here. It was

presently located in the Archeological Museum of Zagreb.

The Byzantine and Frank Rule

After the sons of the Roman Emperor Theodosius, Arcades and Honorees divided the Empire into the East and West in 395 AD, Dalmatia became a part of the Western Empire. In 437 AD Gala Placidia gave away Dalmatia to the Eastern Roman Empire as a wedding gift.

Ivan Duknović, Angel with Torch and coat-of-arms of the ⇨ Cipiko family, 15th C, Trogir Town Museum

Cata Dujšin-Ribar Gallery in the Trogir Town Museum

in Bijaći that in 852 Croatian prince Trpimir issued an official paper, believed to be the first Croatian diplomatic document. The old church that used to be in this area was deconstructed due to archeological excavations. Parts of this structure were then moved to the Museum of the Croatian Archeological Monuments (Muzej hrvatskih arheoloških spomenika) and are being displayed there. In 1908 a new church was built in its place.

National rulers and community leaders occasionally resided in the city itself. In 998 the Venetian duke Peter the Second Orseolus visited the city and found that Svetoslav Suronja, the first born son of King Držislav (*Rex Dalmatiae at Croatiae*), was living there. Svetoslav, who lost his crown as a result of a dispute with his brothers, found refuge in Trogir. He made an alliance with the duke giving him his son Stjepan, who then left for Venice where he married the duke's daughter

Hicela. This was the first in a series of events of neighboring Venice's interference in the city's life. This act created a split in the Držislav dynasty, which in turn caused the end of the independent Croatian State in the late eleventh century.

A few churches or their remains stand as an evidence of this period. Numerous pieces of church remains can be found in the city's lapidary. They are decorated with old Croatian *pleter* (three stranded braid) motif and other ornamentation popular in those times. These decorations can also be found on the walls of houses.

A Part of the Hungaro-Croatian State

After the downfall of the independent Croatian State, Koloman Arpadović was crowned the Hungaro-Croatian king in 1102 in the town of Biograd na moru. In 1107 Koloman gave an oath to Trogir to protect and defend its rights, which

Old town street

Old town street, before The Street of Water

was continued by his descendants. Their gifts of land to the city, church and its nobility expanded the size of Trogir to include Zagora and ensure the town's status of an independent community.

According to the thirteenth century writings of educated bishop and chronicle writer Treguan, the Saraceans burned down Trogir's houses. In those days, the town was surrounded only by drywall, which made it easy for the Venetians to plunder it in 1171 in their search for treasures. The surviving population found refuge in the neighboring Split. During the second half of the twelfth century, life in Trogir returned to normal.

The Hungaro-Croatian King Bela the Fourth took part in a special episode of the Trogir's history. Fleeing the Tartars in 1242, he found refuge in Trogir together with his entire royal entourage. Chronicle writer Toma Arhidjakon wrote that once the Tartars reached the town walls, they, speaking in Croatian, asked Trogirians to surrender the king. Trogirians remained loyal to the king, who rewarded them by confirming their already acquired privileges and giving them more land.

It is important to mention that Trogirian princes were elected by other noblemen from the ranks of the Croatian nobility. This ensured that individuals would not monopolize the rule over the town. This is how the dukes of Bribirski, from the tribe of Šubići, entered the town's political

Medieval House – detail

stage. They played an important role in Trogir's history of the thirteenth and fourteenth century. During the fifteenth century, in order to protect its interests, the community got on the good side of, not only the Hungaro-Croatian crown, but also the Venetians. The nobility sided with the Croatian rulers while the middle class, hoping for a better life, trusted the promising Venetians. In 1322, Trogir shortly puts itself under the protection of Venice, whose interference in the affairs of this independent community became more and more frequent. Trogir, like other Dalmatian cities, acknowledged the rule of King Ludovik Anžuvinski (1342 – 1382) which caused Bijaći to become deserted. Class differences

and animosities caused uprisings of the people in the mid-fourteenth century. There were disagreements between the populace and the nobility as well as between the bishops and the town. Disagreements were based mostly on the rights of gathering income from the agricultural activities, but were also a result of the town's changing political scene when the supporters of the Bosnian king appeared.

The statute of the town of Trogir, written in 1322 and nowadays held in a private collection, regulated legal and public matters of the town and its inhabitants. Ivan Lucić, a famous historian born in Trogir and a father of Croatian historiography, prepared the statute for publishing. Together

Triptych in stone depicting Our Lady, St Jerome and St Ladislav, workshop of Nikola Firentinac (Nicholas of Forence), 15th C, St Lawrence Cathedral

with numerous documents of Trogirian scribes, collected and prepared for publishing by historian don Miho Barada (*Monumenta Traguriensia*), the statue represents a valuable document of the town's medieval history. Reading these documents one can learn many interesting details that characterized the every day life of medieval people. A private collection in Trogir holds the original document from 1271 that writes about magistrate Muccius. It is also the first written manuscript which mentions the Trogir pharmacy as one of the oldest in Croatia.

Trogir boasts two blessed individuals from this period. Augustine Kažotić, the first Croatian Blessed, was a Dominican who attended school in Paris. He was born in Trogir around 1260 and died in Lucera in 1323. His statue, made by sculptor Kruno Bošnjak, was placed in front of the church of St. Dominic (crkva Sv. Dominika) in 2001.

The Blessed Ivan Trogirski (John Ursini), who is considered a saint in Trogir, was a public speaker born in 1032 in Rome. He became the bishop of Trogir in 1062, and remained at this post until his death in 1111. He was sent there by Rome to pacify Trogir's fighting citizens. Since he pacified the situation and turned the ancient town's frictions into peace and harmony, the grateful

Detail of the portal of the Cega Family Palace

town people wrote on the coffin containing his relics: DA PACEM FILLIS TUIS (Cathedral of St. Lawrence). Trogir celebrates this saint twice a year. The first holiday is on November 14th which is also the Day of the town of Trogir, and a church holiday. The second celebration, called *primišćenje* (the transfer) and taking place on May 4th, is a remembrance of that day in 1681 when the saint's relics were transferred to the Trogir's present day main church.

The Venetian Rule

In the year of 1403, Ladislav Napuljski was crowned Hungaro-Croatian king in Zadar. In 1409, after six years of his rule, he sold Dalmatia to Venice. After days of resistance, on June 22nd, 1420 Trogir fell into the hands of Venetian troops led by Captain Pietro Loredano. It is noteworthy to mention that Trogir women, together with their husbands, participated in defense of the town. Afterwards, they stubbornly continued to cherish Croatian customs and use the Croatian language, even though the official language was Italian. Many citizens of Trogir were dissatisfied with the Venetian rule and resisted it, while others left for neighboring Croatia. Lives of many disobedient

Nikola Firentinac, bas-relief with the figure of Alviz Cipiko (Coriolanus' son), 15th C, Small Cipiko Palace

Trogirian nobles were endangered. One of them was Petar Berislavić, the Croatian *ban* (deputy prince) and bishop. He was born in Trogir in the house that has been preserved to the present day. Berislavić, asking the pope and the European countries for help, tried to liberate Trogir from Venetian rule. To no avail, he died fighting the Turks in 1520. The people of Trogir lived an uneasy life due to Turkish invasions from the second half of the fifteenth century until the Turks were pushed inland at the end of the seventeenth century.

During the times of Venetian control, the rule was in the hands of the duke. He was responsible to the general governor (providur) in Zadar, who in turn was elected from the ranks of Venetian nobles. The duke and his family resided in the communal palace. To attend church festivities he would enter the cathedral building through the side door, called the duke's door. Upper, Lower and Secret committee ruled the city together with the duke. During the rule of Duke Nicholas Micheli, in 1517, Trogir was minting its own currency (called *bagattino*) out of pure copper and imprinted with a face of the town's patron saint, St. Lovro.

Trogir flourished during the Renaissance period. Its biggest financial contribution was made by its middle class, as Venice and other powers that ruled the town were only interested in exploiting it. During the Renaissance period begins a lively and diverse building development of the town. Serenissima used this to show its power and nobility its wealth. They competed in building glamorous villas. This competition would sometimes cause "heads to roll", such as in the case of Šimun Sobota who was killed by his neighbor Marin Andreis. Shortly following this incident, Šobota's son was killed and their family left without an heir. One of Trogir's legendary pieces, the sarcophagus with "mercy" (prepared by Ante Ivančić) vividly describes this tragedy.

During the time of the Renaissance, the nobility reads Roman classics, writes, collects books for their libraries, gathers domestic and foreign artists and building Masters. The nobles worked on making their town into environment with cultural ambiance. Koriolan Cipiko, a humanist and warrior, published an incunabula *Petri Mocenici imperatotis gesta* (De bello Asiatico – About the Asian War). During the fifteenth century, Hvar poet Hanibal Lucić wrote poems dedicated to Milica and her Cipiko family. They provided refuge for him when he escaped from Hvar during the people's uprising on this

Nikola Firentinac, Angel, 15th C, St Lawrence Cathedral

island. The Cipiko's library contained a hand written document *Cena Trimalchionis*, which is a section of the novel *Satirkon* written by the Roman writer Petronio Arbitro (in Paris from 1703, Bibliothque nationale – codex Traguriensis, Parisinus, number 7989.) Petar Lucić, the father of famous Ivan, gathered the first collection of Croatian poems (called *Vartal*) written by old writers. Vartal used to be kept in the Monastery

Southern Town Gate, 16th C

of St. Nicholas (sv. Nikole) and is now located in Croatian Archeological Foundation (HAZ - Hrvatski Arheološki Zavod). The Organization Matica Hrvatska Trogir today publishes a magazine that bears the same name. Ivan Lucić

Kamerlengo Tower – detail, 15th C

⇦ *Blessed Ivan Trogirski holding the scale-model of the town of Trogir, 15th C, St Lawrence Cathedral, Collection of artefacts*

wrote the first academically significant history of Croatia and Dalmatia as well as his home town of Trogir (De regno Dalmatiae at Criatiae, Memorie storiche di ragurio ora dello Trau). In his research, he relied on available historical sources and written documents. During the same time, his fellow citizen Pavao Andreis wrote his version of the history of Trogir.

Like in other Dalmatian cities and towns, the common folk of Trogir gathered in organizations called *bratovštine* (fraternities). These were generally church organizations with a social and humanitarian purpose. Every trade had its own fraternity that protected its interests, and was aligned with a particular church. Different social classes entertained themselves as their income and resources allowed. The nobility attended theater, concerts, balls organized in private villas… The common folk entertained themselves on the streets, and used the cathedral to hold various performances. St. Mark's day was a big festivity in Trogir, when the town would be filled with people form Zagorje. They would come to town bringing with them their customs, and would greet the duke and the flag of St. Mark which would hang on *štandarac* (the year of 1605).

Venetian power started to wane in the eighteenth century, the strength of its rule started to diminish, and it struggled to remain afloat. Unrest began on June 14th in the turbulent year of 1797. The Venetian rule ended in anarchy; wild masses of bitter people rebelled, killing many and plundering rich homes. After almost four hundred years of the Venetian rule, this "lion" disappeared from the political arena. All the Venetian rulers were removed from their posts in Trogir by 1932 when fascism and its motto of "which ever place bears a sign of lion with wings, it should belong to Italy" started to spread across Italy.

After a month of anarchy, the Austrian general of Croatian background Mate Rukavina came to Trogir. On July 9th 1797 he gave a speech in Croatian in the Trogir Cathedral. The representatives who went to Vienna to demand the union of Croatia and Dalmatia were supported by the people of Trogir, however the Austrian government felt this request was too premature. The first Austrian administration was established and lasted until 1806.

The Beginning of the Nineteenth Century – the French Rule

The French took over the control of Trogir in 1806. The town, together with the entire surrounding area, became a part of the Napoleon's Kingdom of Italy. Its capital of Milan was responsible for appointing the province head for Dalmatia. The first appointee Vicenzo Dandolo came on an official visit to Trogir on September

Trogir quay ⇨

9th 1806, and was cordially greeted by the town and church administration and some of the common folk. In the beginning of the French rule, the church got the short end of the stick since the French soldiers, upon entering the town, moved into the Monastery of St. Dominic. The monastery was spared from destruction by the devoted Dominicans who remained living in the choir loft.

When they got used to the new administration, the people of Trogir began organizing festivities celebrating Napoleon's victories across Europe. One of such festivities began on an early morning with the ringing of the church bells and the arrival of festively dressed Zagorci. Festively decorated ships were anchored in the harbor, while all the shops and houses were adorned with tapestries and flowers. Cannons were shooting, and there was a special sung mass in the church. The town was overflowing with people walking from the main square, where they would sing and dance, to the harbor where a regatta (sailing competition) was taking place.

After establishing their rule over the town, the French

Nikola Firentinac, mourning ⇨
of Christ, 15th C

Bell-tower of St Lawrence Cathedral, detail of the second floor, 15th C

started to modernize it. The swamps in the town's vicinity as well as ponds on Soline were drained. The use of Ošljak well was permitted only for animals, while its prior use as a source of potable water and for washing clothes was prohibited. The French built roads that connected the town and the surrounding area, therefore the road to Zagora was named Napoleon's road. They also tried to revive the economy by publishing guides on the use of new agricultural methods. As a result, representatives lead by Luka Garagnin were sent to Paris to give their greetings to Napoleon and convince him that the Dalmatians were loyal to the French rule.

The French immediately started promoting and supporting the school attendance by both girls and boys. The college of St. Lazarus (Kolegij Sv. Lazara) was successfully operating from 1802 in the facilities of monastery on the island of Čiovo. It was headed by Ivan Skakoca, who in 1806 became its head master, and the college became an institution of higher learning. Trogirian doctor Jakov Mirković taught medicine classes there for a few years.

In 1808, the military ruler of Dalmatia, August Marmont, ordered the construction of a monument symbolizing the gratitude to France. This monument called *Marmontov gloriet* was never finished. During the French rule, all the civil marriages took place in front of it, but these acts were often made fun of by the people. As this monument was obstructing the building of the soccer stadium in the second half of the twentieth century, it was transferred to its present day location.

Very briefly, in 1809, Trogir accepted without resistance the Austrian troops. They consisted mostly of Croatians and were lead by general Stojčević. General administrator (providur) Vincenzo Dandolo left to a new post, while Marshal Marmont who was beloved mostly

among the people established peace in the town. During his administration the tidiness of the town had a high priority. Twice a day, at the sound of the church bell, every citizen was required to clean up the area in front of his house, otherwise a penalty was imposed. All the meat shops located in the city center were transferred to buildings on the waterfront. Deteriorating towers which did not serve any purpose were removed.

All these things prove that during the brief rule of the French, which lasted until 1814, they attempted to modernize the town.

Courtyard with the well crown of previous St Peter's Monastery

St Mark's Tower, 15th C, today House of Dalmatian Brass Band

The Period of the Austrian Rule

In the beginning of its rule (which began in 1814 and lasted until 1918) the Austrian government respected the existing administration of Trogir. The same was the case in Split. After the 1815 Vienna Congress, Dalmatia was given to Austria. Trogir became a part of the Split district whose administration and judiciary were combined into one body. The district administration performed judicial duties while political work was performed by special offices called political praetorships. County administration was formed in Trogir and was headed by a supervisor.

Austria developed a unique book of land titles and deeds for entire Croatia and in 1830 the state land office was established for the entire county of Trogir. During this time the town was barely surviving. Many economic activities ceased while, as a result of political changes, the once ruling nobility lost its privileges and became poor.

In the second half of the nineteenth century, as a result of new, revitalizing ideas the political scene in Trogir became livelier. The landowner named Antun Fanfogna who was heading the autonomy (autonomasku) party was the town's mayor until the people's party took over. The center of the awakened national conciseness was Narodna štionica (National reading library) established in 1867. Its first benefactor was Croatian bishop

Gloriette from the time of French administration, 19th C

Josip Juraj Strossmayer. The people's movement among the Trogir's population prevailed in 1870's but it was not until 1886 that the movement, lead by the first people's mayor Špiro Puović, finally scored a victory. According to their statutes of 1871, during the time of the Renaissance, autonomy and people's parties had their own bands. During the second half of the nineteenth century education system also flourished and the elementary school was established. The school later developed into a high school.

After all these turbulent years, the beautification and development of the town began. Deteriorating buildings were torn down and new ones were built in their place. When the harbor was restored and expanded, one section of the medieval town was lost forever. The Trogir born engineer Josip Slade who worked in many other cities, worked on these projects in his home town.

The nineteenth century Trogir lived through periods of deterioration, renovation and change, all of which permanently changed the appearance of the town, as well as the consciousness, life and customs of its citizens.

The Twentieth Century

The beginning of the twentieth century began with the construction of new buildings on the foundations of earlier structures. Don Frane Bulić, who was active in conserving the monuments of cultural heritage, helped develop this consciousness among the people of Trogir. Another individual who also greatly contributed to this effort was Roko Slade Šilović. The everyday life resembled in a way that of the end of the previous century. As the nobility lost its power, the common people took over leading positions, even in organizations such as the Croatian People's Education Society by the name of Berislavić. The town strove to have a train stop on the railroad going to Split and a blueprint was drawn for the construction of a train station. With the end of the Austrian rule in the year of 1918, came the end of the so called Austrian way of life.

The First World War had an exhausting effect on the people of Trogir who found themselves defending the Austrian interests. After the end of the Austrian rule, supporters of Italy attempted to establish the rule by the Kingdom of Italy, but without success.

The period of the Kingdom of Slovenes, Croats and Serbs, followed by the Kingdom of Yugoslavia was characterized by political turmoil. Political issues revolved around the rule over the city and the so called agrarian question. During this time the way of thinking and speaking as well as the way of life changed. The first public fountain was built in 1930. Sewage system and running water were added in 1936 using the water supply from the spring of the Jadro River. Electricity was also installed in 1930. Some families found a new source of income by opening up shops. This activity created a new class of well to do people, in addition to entrepreneurs and peasants. During this time ship building developed, and so did the processing and exports of herbs and plants especially unbleached cotton fabrics. The early 1930's witnessed the arrival of first Czech and Slovak tourists which lead to the boom of tourism in Trogir.

Alessandro Vittoria, Statue of Apostle Matthews, 16th C, bell-tower of St Lawrence Cathedral

Politics played an important role even in those days. As the agrarian question remained unresolved, it was the main point of contention among various political parties fighting for power. The leading party that won the 1935 election was the Croatian People's Party. Communists successfully infiltrated this party and as a result of the popularity the People's Party enjoyed, they managed to win the township elections which took place in the beginning of the Second World War.

During the Second World War, after the collapse of the Kingdom of Yugoslavia in 1941, Mussolini's army entered Trogir. They tried to destroy everything that was Croatian, taking down

Town vistas

Croatian historic monuments. As a result, after Italy capitulated, the people massively joined the Partisan antifascist movement. There were also those who joined the ranks of the Independent State of Croatia (NDH). The Partisan troops entered Trogir in the year of 1944.

The period of the Federal People Republic, followed by the Socialist Federal Republic of Yugoslavia was characterized by big changes in the way of life. After purges and punishment of those who did not share the same ideology, the life resumed a more normal tone. Since Yugoslavia was a socialist country, agricultural activity suffered from industrialization. Large hotels were built to accommodate the new trend of mass tourism, ship building industry was strengthened, and many monuments were renovated by special services for conservation.

At the end of the century, in 1990, Croatia finally became an independent state again. Members of the Trogirian families perished in the war of invasion against Croatia (known as the Homeland War). As privatization took place, small privately owned shops started to open up, as well as other small businesses.

In comparison to many other turbulent periods when Trogir was unfortunately ruled by some foreign power, this town of continuous history entered the twenty first century as a part of independent Croatia.

CULTURAL HERITAGE AND THE ARTS

Forts and Towers

Trogir was founded on an island whose shape and topography influenced the look and appearance of the town walls. Unlike the walls surrounding towns on flat land that are easily designed and built, the Trogir's walls vary in size and style. In the prehistoric times the walls were most likely ellipse shaped, as this was common among the forts of the Illyrian settlements. The twelfth century attacks from the sea resulted in the destruction of these walls and it was not until the early 1200's that they were rebuilt. Since this time, except for a few minor moves and additions, the walls remained on the same location.

The walls used to have two gates: the South gate leading to the sea and the North gate leading to the mainland. During the Greek times both were moved to the spot east of the present day gates. The new gate (also called the port gate) was built in the Middle Ages, more precisely in 1593, next to the church of St. Dujmo (crkva sv. Dujma). The gate exemplifies manneristic style and still has the original wooden planks with metal nails. A small enclosure can be found next to the gate which was used as a shelter by those travelers who found themselves locked out after the town gates were closed up at night. The North gate was also moved east, next to the old stone bridge. After the bridge was torn down in the seventeenth century, the gate was moved to its present day location. The gate is known for the statue of the town's protector, the Blessed Ivan Trogirian (Ivan Orsini) which hovers over it. It is interesting to mention that from the mid 1600s to the beginning of the First World War there used to be a pine tree growing out of a crack in the stone. There used to be a small gate on the western side of the old town walls, near the church of Our Lady of Karmel (crkva Gospe od Karmela). It was most likely used for taking out the garbage.

As houses started to be built in the new part of town, the walls had to be enlarged. As early as 1289 the Burg neighborhood of Trogir was entirely encircled by the walls. In the early 1400s as people were fleeing from the Turks they found refuge in Trogir. At this time Burg got its new name - Novi grad (New Town).

Saint-protector of the town, Blessed Ivan Trogirski, the work of Bonino from Milan, 15th C, Northern Town Gate

Kamerlengo Tower, 15th C

The tower by the name of Veriga Tower (Kula od veriga) was built in 1380 by people from Genoa. It was later enlarged and the fortress of Kamerlengo was added to this structure. The fortress was built from 1420 to 1437 by Master Marin Radoj. Its name comes from the Latin word camerarius, meaning treasury clerk, a person who was responsible for performing all financial activities requested by the duke. The fortress was surrounded by a ditch and was filled with sand. Inside the fort was a well and a few other small structures including a chapel and residential quarters. For strategic and security reasons, the complex could function as a miniature town, in case an uprising took place. The North-Western tower was surrounded by a mound called zetto which was made of small stones. Its function was to prevent galleys and boats from approaching the tower. The main entrance to the tower was located on its northern side and has remained there to this day.

Across from it, to the North is the fort of St. Mark (kula sv. Marka) built in the fifteenth century during the Venetian rule. Today "The House of Dalmatian Music").

Throughout the 1800's fortresses and towers were demolished as they were preventing the spreading of the town and fresh air from entering its narrow streets and houses. As the look of Trogir changed, so did the life of people living in it. The Medieval Trogirian lived in a town surrounded by town walls.

At night, Trogir was scarcely lit, and although this might seem very romantic, it was a rather mystical sight. This is likely the reason how folk tales of ghosts, ferries and the so called macarolčići

Small loggia, 15th C, shelter for delayed passengers after closing the gate of the medieval town

spread. These were ferry tale creatures, believed to be the spirits of dead children bearing animal features, always present and ready for mischief.

The Austrian army also used the old town walls. After the Austrian rule the walls became the county's property and were mainly used for storage. The St. Mark's Fort was at one time used as a public slaughter house.

The construction of the waterfront was finished in the early 1900s. The building sheltering hospital offices was taken down, and other old structures were replaced by new ones. The new school building was competed in 1909 and is still being used for the needs of Trogir's elementary school. The new court house was built in 1910 at a location where old bishop palace used to stand before it burned down. The court house consists of a realistically reconstructed bishop's tower.

The Vitturi tower has also been preserved as a part of the women's Benedictine monastery of St. Nicholas (samostan Sv. Nikole).

It is located on the eastern side of the present day town gate. On the western side is the tower of St. Nicholas.

The Kamerlengo fortress started to deteriorate in the early twentieth century, but was renovated after the Second World War.

It is being used as a summer stage and movie theatre at night. During the day it is a sight seeing spot as it offers beautiful views of the entire surrounding area. There are no visible remains of other fortresses.

The town walls remained standing only in a few spots such as near the South town gates, on the Western and Easter side of town, in the North next to the church of Our Lady of Karmel, and near the town gates.

CHURCHES

Churches Near the Northern Town Gates

The Church of St. Leo is located near the North gate leading to the mainland. It was originally dedicated to St. Leo, then St. Nicholas and finally to St. Barbara.

It is speculated that the original building was constructed in the 1100s.

During the eighteenth century it was used as a gun powder storage, at the end of the nineteenth century it was a blacksmith shop and in the early twentieth century it was reconstructed as a residential building.

Churches on the Town Square and its Vicinity

The cathedral of St. Lovro - John (katedrala sv. Lovre - Ivana) holds a special place among the historical monuments of Trogir. It is not only important as a church, but also has architectural

Radovan's portal – lunette, 13th C, St Lawrence Cathedral

⇦ *St Lawrence Cathedral*

value that exemplifies many building styles, from the Romanesque to Baroque. It also holds valuable works of art. During the Medieval times the cathedral was a place where the living would come to honor the dead. Its construction began around the year 1200 and was completed in the beginning of seventeenth century. The church steeple took almost 200 years to build. It went through a series of changes in the eighteenth century when it was consecrated once again following a fire that destroys numerous documents in the bishop's archives. The long period of its construction can be seen in the variety of building styles used on its bell tower. The first floor of the tower was built in Gothic style, while the second shows the Flowering Gothic style characteristic of the Venetian times of the fifteenth century. The third floor, which was completed in the late 1500s, is decorated in the Renaissance style of Trifun Bokanić. The last pyramid shaped floor has four statues made by Alessandro Vittorio, and have been replaced with replicas. A gold, metal ball, which was recently restored to its previous condition, stands on top of the bell tower. It contains relics of saints which were to protect the people of Trogir.

The atrium of the cathedral has two entrances. On the left hand side of the Western entrance are stairs leading to a terrace. The terrace is leaning against the church's front façade decorated with a Gothic rosetta window. The fifteenth century baptistery was made by Albanian artist Andrija Aleši. He is also the author of the Christ's Baptism relief located near the entrance and the St. Jerolim in a Cave relief found inside the church. The church has a floor plan with right angles, its ceiling is decorated with angels carrying a wreath. This detail shows obvious influence of Nikola Florentinac. A stone baptistery, covered with a wooden cover held by statutes of two angles, stands in the center of the church.

Radovan's portal – detail, St Lawrence Cathedral

⇦ *Radovan's portal – detail, St Lawrence Cathedral*

Radovan's portal – detail,
St Lawrence Cathedral

⇦ *Radovan's portal – detail, St Lawrence Cathedral*

KRSTIONICA
DIE TAUFKAPELLE
THE BAPTISTERY
IL BATTISTERO
LE BAPTISTÈRE
EL BAPTISTERIO

Baptistery – interior, St Jerome in the Cave, work by Aleši, 15th C, St Lawrence Cathedral

As early as 1240, the Western portal, also known as Radovan's portal was made and was enlarged by Radovan's workers in the late 1200s. The year of its making and the author's name can be clearly seen on the lower part of lunett. The lunett shows the Nativity of Christ (on its front side and on the back side, later covered with the organ, is a cross), the Voyage of the Three Wise Men and the Adoration of Shepherds. At each end in the lower part of the arch are: Annunciation, Adoration of Kings, and Joseph's Dream. The outside arch show the scenes from Christ's life: Escape to Egypt, Christ's Temptation in the Dessert, Entrance to Jerusalem, Washing of Feet, Apprehension and Whipping of Christ, Crucifixion and Resurrection. Figures of lions, acting the role of protectors, are visible on the left and right side while above them stands the figures of Adam and Eve. The first set of pillars on the left and right side shows figures of the twelve Apostles. The second row depicts the calendar months and various works that is performed during each season. The third row of small round columns portrays scenes from every

⇦ *Baptistery, bas-relief above the entrance – Andrija Aleši, Christ's baptizing, 15th C, St Lawrence Cathedral*

Interior of the three-aisled Trogir cathedral ⇨

Detail of the pulpit in the Trogir cathedral

day life and ferry tale creatures. In the lower part are eight figures wearing different Mediterranean folk costumes while telamons (male figures) are functioning as carriers of the portal. The face of St. Lovro is at the top of the portal, and although the church was dedicated to his name, people usually call it the church of St. John. The people of Trogir gave the Blessed John a special place in their town by building a chapel to which they transferred his remains. Master Radovan was the most famous example of the Croatian Medieval sculptors. Certain experts believe that his sculpting style can be recognized on some pieces in the St. Mark's basilica in Venice. It is believed that sculptures located inside the round windows above the portal have also been made by Radovan. The sculpture on the right hand side depicts beasts drinking out of a goblet, while that on the

Blaž Jurjev Trogiranin, Crucifixion,
15th C, St Lawrence Cathedral

54

left portrays Lust, as a woman being eaten by dragons.

The portal leads to the interior of a three-naval church with narrow Romanesque windows and three semicircular apses on the eastern side. The middle one displays the main altar above which stands a ciborium with sculptures of the Virgin and angel Gabriel in the scene of Annunciation. It was made in the fourteenth century by Master Mavro, and the restoration in 2001 discovered its original gold leaf. During the Baroque, a marble tabernacle was added to the altar, but was later moved to the chapel of St. Jerome (sv. Jerolim). Two statues of Blessed John and St. Lovro were also added. The wooden choir pews were decorated by Ivan Budislavić in the fifteenth century. The octagonal preaching post is decorated with Romanesque capitals which were gold plated at one time. Above it stands a sculpture of the Cross which was made around 1440 by Blaž Jurjev Trogiranin. On each side of the crucified statue of Jesus stand figures of Evangelists. A large fourteenth century wooden chandelier, in a shape of the Greek cross, stands in the center of the church. It used to be lit with oil, but now runs on electricity. People of Trogir ordered it to be made and to

Bartolomeo Coda, Christ's Baptizing, 16th C, St Lawrence Cathedral

resemble a similar one in the church of St. Mark's in Venice.

The organ is placed along the Western wall, and the original one was made in 1485 by Father Urbin. Later on a new Baroque choir was build with an organ made by Gaettan Callido. Some written sources explain that Dominik Moscatelli made a smaller organ which was built into the one made by Callido. This old organ was destroyed during January of 1940 and Milan Majdak was made responsible for building a new one. He used all the parts of the previous organ so that the new instrument preserved the warm, festive sound.

The most beautiful parts of the church have to be the chapel of Blessed John, the mausoleum and the church hall. The chapel was built in the 1400s following the floor plan designed by Nikola Firentinac and artistic guidance of Andrija Alešija and Ivan Duknović. It resembles the Antiquity style, showing the underworld life depicted by winged boys carrying torches on their way out of it. The earthly life is portrayed by a scene of Apostles being led by Jesus. The round windows characterize the Sun, the ceiling in whose center stands the painting of God, portrays the sky. During the Baroque, statues of marble angles, made

Chapel of Blessed Ivan Trogirski, 15th C, work of Nikola Firentinac, Andrija Aleši and Ivan Duknović, St Lawrence Cathedral

Chapel of Blessed Ivan Trogirski – detail, 15th C, St Lawrence Cathedral

Chapel of Blessed Ivan Trogirski – detail, Spiritello, the boy who comes from the underground with a torch, St Lawrence Cathedral

by Jerolim Diogene, were added to the altar. The bust of God made by Firentinac was replaced by a work of Macanović (Ignacije).

The side naves are decorated with altars. The Gothic chapel of St. Jerome has a beautiful tabernacle located to the left of the entrance. Next to it stands the altar of Annunciation also known as the altar of Mary. Adjacent to it is the chapel of St. John. The altar of the Holy Cross is located in the apses to the left of the main altar. To the right of the entrance stands the altar of St. Augustine and next to it the Jubilee altar. At the end of the twentieth century the bust of Blessed Alojzije Stepinac was put up between them. The altar of Our Lady of Mercy can be found in the apses to the right of the main altar. Close to it is also a well and a plaque

St Lawrence Cathedral – Collection of Artefacts

Bishops' mitre

Hands, relics of Blessed Ivan Trogirski, 15th C

Signet-ring of Trogir chapter, 14th C

Reliquary, Angel with the hand of Blessed Ivan Trogirski, 17th C

Silver jugg, 14th C

Cross from Avignon, 14th C

Hood with the image of St Martin and a Bagger, 15th St Lawrence Cathedral

Small altar from ivory, workshop of Embriachi, 15th C, St Lawrence Cathedral – Collection of Artefacts

marking a spot where the ancient tomb of Blessed Ivan was found. The pillars of the main nave, just like the side altars, are decorated with art-work of prominent painters.

The sacristy, built in the mid fifteenth century stores the cathedral's treasures, such as gifts received throughout centuries, from its founding to the present day, most of which were given by Croatian kings and nobility. Some of the pieces are exhibited inside the fifteenth century carved cabinets made by Grgur Vidov. Above them stand the coats of arms of bishops who presided over the bishopric town until it was abolished in 1828. The papal bull Locum Beati Petri, on June 30th of that year abolished the Trogir bishopric and merged it with the Splitsko-Makarska one.

One of the most interesting pieces of all embroidered textiles exhibited in the sacristy is the fourteenth century hooded cape portraying the scene of St. Martin with a beggar. Tradition has it that it was a gift from Bella the Fourth. Other pieces include: dalmatics (robes worn by bishops) and missals from the sixteenth century, the fourteenth century miter (a liturgical headdress) of Trogirian Bishop Kažotić, the stamp of Trogir bishopric from 1300s, fourteenth century silver pitcher, miniature ebony altar, the Embriachi workshop from 1400s, reliquary of Blessed Ivan Trogirian, the fourteenth century Crucifix from Avignon, and many others. All of the described pieces, as well as the one from the gallery , have been restored in 2001 in order to be included in the exhibit called The Art Treasure of Croatia – Trogir 1200 to 1600. It was held in the church of San Barnaba in Venice from June 9th to November 4th, 2001.

The adjacent structure built in the Neogothic style in the mid-nineteenth century contains a valuable and rich bishopric library on its first floor. It holds about 3000 works, a valuable archive collection as well as a collection of old hand written documents belonging to the period from the twelfth to eighteenth century. One of these documents published on June 23, 1795 is very important for the history of Trogir's music heritage as it permitted the reading of the first Christmas mass before midnight. This custom has been preserved to the present day, and a celebratory mass, whose music was composed by author Ivan Bozzotti, is sung in Latin every Christmas season.

The church of St. Mary (crkva sv. Marije), built in the ninth century used to have a six apsidas, floor plan and cupola. Unfortunately, due to the danger of its cupola collapsing, the church was torn down in 1851. Today, its remains which can be found in the vicinity of the town square are clearly visible. Remains include those of the church walls, while one of its apses was discovered inside the wall of the neighboring church, St. Sebastian's, during its renovation. Archeological excavations discovered a gable, on which the formula supporting the advocate's argument was written. The partially reconstructed gable can be found in the lapidary of the Museum of the Town of Trogir. The 1757 graphics of artist C.L. Clerisseau (Ermitage in Petrograd) forever preserved the image of this church.

The church of St. Sebastian with the clock tower was constructed around 1476. It was built by the town people as vow of their gratitude to St. Sabastian who was believed to have saved them from the plague. The church has a

Church of St Barbara (St Martin), 11th C – interior

Remnants of the church of St Mary, 9th C

60

Blaž Jurjev Trogiranin, Polyptych – Our Lady with Saints, 15th C

Blaž Jurjev Trogiranin, Polyptych – St Jacob with Saints, 15th C

Blaž Jurjev Trogiranin, Our Lady in Rose Garden, 15th C

Ivan Duknović, Our Lady, 15th C

simple layout, a semicircular apse facing South, and due to its eastern wall leaning against the neighboring church of St. Mary, the entrance is on the Northern side. It has a Renaissance façade, made by the workshop of Nikola Firentinac. After St. Mary's was torn down, some of its decorative elements were incorporated into walls of the church of St. Sebastian. It was turned into a storage facility in 1850, and pieces of the main altar were transferred to the town lapidary. Recent excavations discovered the church's original floor while underneath it were found three sarcophagi. They were discovered laying around the walls of St. Mary's atrium and are nowadays on display in an exhibition room.

When St. Sebastian's was renovated, partial reconstruction of the altar was performed, including the statue of St. Sebastian made by Nikola Firentinac. Today, the renovated church commemorates the Fallen Soldiers of the Croatian Homeland War, 1991-1995.

The church of St. Barbara, also known as St. Martina's was built in Early Romanesque style in the eleventh century. Its wall borders the town square. Inside the church stands a stone beam bearing the text about the restorer Peter and his wife Dobrica. The beam is an obvious reminded of the church that was reconstructed into the present day St. Barbara's. The church entrance is decorated with a motif of three crosses, enfolded in

Pinakoteka - Collection of sacred artefacts, St Lawrence Cathedral

a three stranded braid and surrounded by symbolic shapes and figures. This detail used to belong to the previous church. Pieces of Antiquity remains, such as pillars and capitals, were used to build the church of St. Barbara. It has a three naves build with three apses on the eastern side and a bell tower in the middle of its cupola. There are narrow niches on the side walls. There used to be another church of St. Barbara, located on the main land. However, it was torn down in 1647 in order to eliminate any building that the Turks might have used for defensive purposes. Prior to its destruction, the church's altar was first moved to the church of St. Lav and then to St. Martin's. Its three altars were once used by soldiers for mounting cannons. In the mid nineteenth century, St. Barbara's was used as a kitchen and storage, and was made into the lapidary at the end of the nineteenth century. It was restored for the first time in 1931 and again in the late 1980s. Above the main altar hangs the painting of St. Barbara, a copy of the original work

by Palmo the Older found in the church of St. Mary Formosa in Venice.

The church of St. John the Baptist was built in the thirteenth century and used to be an integral part of the male Benedictine monastery whose buildings stretched to the North of the church. Archeological excavations in the area between the church and the Town Hall found remains of an earlier Benedictine monastery complex, which lead to a conclusion that in the Early Christian period there used to be another church in the place of St. John's. Remains of that church's apses have been reconstructed on the floor. St. John's was built in Romanesque style, it has one nave and the belfry. The portal holds a sculpture of the Lamb of God made in the style of Master Radovan. It shares the same architectural details with the cathedral. The church was closed down in the mid nineteenth century and was at one time used for depositing stones. In the early 1900s, due to the efforts of the society for Preservation of

Monuments Radovan, the church was renovated. Renovations lasted until after the Second World War when the stones were moved to the cloister of the Dominican monastery. The fourteenth century tomb stone bearing the figure of priest Savin and many frescos are found in the church. The most valuable piece of the stone collection include the relief with the scene of Mourning of Christ, a work of Nikola Firentinac.

The gallery collection of sacral artifacts belonging to the cathedral of St Lawrence was opened to the public in 2005, and it is now situated in the house of the priest not far from the church of St John the Baptist. One enters the new Museum from the square through the remnants of the partly reconstructed early Croatian six-leaf church of St Mary. The ground-floor is partly used for the museum needs and partly as a multi-purpose hall. These two areas are linked with reconstructed stone door frames that were before the decorations for the church of the Holy Spirit. New wooden doorframes are made according to the model of the original ones from the Garagnin-Fanfogna Palace.

One ascends the stone staircase to the permanent exhibition divided in three halls. The Crucifixion with the triumphant Christ from the 14th C from the church of St Andrew, and the altar painting with the scene of St Andrew and saints (also 14th C) by a disciple of Paolo Veneziano dominate the first hall. The following artifacts were brought from the Cathedral: Our Lady with the Child (15th C) by Quirizio da Murano, doorframes of an old organ, one depicting St Jerome and another St John the Baptist, both by Gentile Bellini. Also there were the parts of the wooden painted cupboard of the cathedral organ from the second half of the 16th century. The other hall is devoted to the paintings by Blaž Jurjev Trogiranin from the 15th century: the Crucifixion (the church of Our Lady of Carmel), a polyptych depicting St Jacob with

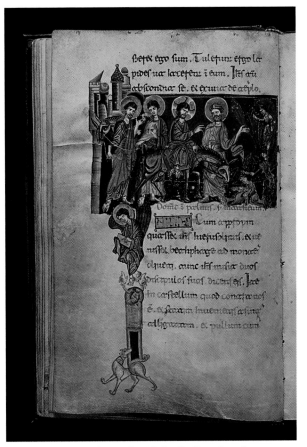

Trogir – Gospel Book, 13th C, Pinakoteka - Collection of sacred Artefacts, St Lawrence Cathedral

saints with the signature of the artist (the church of St Jacob on Čiovo), Our Lady in the Rose Garden (Cathedral), a polyptych depicting Our Lady with the child and saints (the church of St John the Baptist). The written heritage is exhibited in the continuing corridor (Evangelical Book, 13th C, Beneventana, Psalter, 15th C in Gothic letters, Matrix List of the Brotherhood of the Holy Spirit, 15th C, illustrated by Blaž Jurjev Trogiranin, the Petar Cipiko Codex, 15th C. The third hall housed the polyptych that was before on the high altar (13th C); it was used as the raw material for the choir stools of the Cathedral in the 15th C, and

Church of St Nicholas (St Dujam), founded in 1064 - interior

depicts Our Lady with the Child and saints, a work from a Dalmatian painting workshop.

The relief with the scene of Our Lady with the child, by the Hvar sculptor Ivan Duknović is only temporarily exhibited here. Its permanent place is envisaged in the Museum of the Town of Trogir where Our Lady will be joined by Duknović's puto with the coat of arts of the Cipiko family. This Museum will then exhibit three Duknović's works (together with the lunette with the coat of arms of the Cipiko family) from the total of six preserved in the town of Trogir (Cathedral – the chapel of Ivan Trogirski: St Thomas and St John the Evangelist; the Franciscan monastery of St Anthony on Čiovo: the statue of St Magdalene).

The church of St. Steven the Martyr (crkva sv. Stjepana Prvomučenika) was believed to have been very old. It had an arch, four pillars and two altars dedicated to St. Steven and St. Mary of Loretta. It was torn down in 1769 and a new

⇦ *St Sebastian, work of Nikola Firentinac, 15th C, Church of St Sebastian*

Collection of Artefacts Kairos within the monastery of St Nicholas

church was built with efforts from the Trogir bishopric. There is a tablet on one pillar below the new organ that testifies to this. The old church of St. Steven was most likely located in the vicinity of the town square since.

Churches by the Coast

The church of St. Nicholas, also known as the church of St. Dujam, with the art collection Kairos is a part of the only preserved Benedictine monastery for women. It was established in 1064 specifically for noble women. One of the late

Antiquity forts is now the northern wall of the church, while a newer fort makes up its southern wall. This creates a very unique building – church within forts. It was constructed on the foundations of older churches and remains of the Southern town gates of ancient Tragurium. It was built in a variety of styles, from the Romanesque to Baroque. Its northern wall bears an Early Romanesque relief with figures of the Lamb of God, St. Benedict and St. Scolastic. Another relief whose author was Nikola Firentinac, is located next to it and portrays St. Nicholas. At the end of the sixteenth century

67

Collection of Artefacts Kairos within the monastery of St Nicholas

Polyptych, 15th C

Milica Cipiko had a bell tower built decorated with lace-like stone grid which was made by the carver family of Trifun Bokanić from the island of Brač. The church has a Baroque interior, decorated with stucco walls and portraits of saints painted by Nicola Grassi. These paintings are nowadays in the monastery collection. Above the main altar hangs a semicircular canvas picturing the scene of Golgotha, into which a wooden, polychrome Crucifix is incorporated. Paintings by nineteenth century artist Antonio Zuccara hang above the side altars. A Greek tablet from the second century BC, which lists the names of people performing public duties, can be found on the southern wall of the monastery's courtyard. The small space used as a lapidary exhibits numerous stones and tablets, such as the one on the Eastern wall which describes how Teodor Vitturi, by request from *ban* Berislavić, received from King Ludovik the Second a permit for building four mills on Pantan. This is a written proof that in those days the Croatian land used to stretch all the way to Trogir.

Crucifixion, workshop of Paolo Veneziano, 14th C

Unknown painter, Our Lady with the Child, St John the Baptist, St Sebastian and St Rocco, 16th C

Blaž Jurjev Trogiranin, Our Lady with the Child, St Francis and St Catharine, 15th C

of the Kairos building (which used to belong to the Statilic family). The deity warns people that they need to be aware that happiness exists before it is too late to enjoy it. Kairos is often used as Trogir's Mascot. Archeological excavations inside the church found a third century relief of Achilles. The oldest sacral painting of Trogir is the Virgin Mary with the Child which dates to the late 1200s. There are other paintings of this kind, such as those believed to have been made by artists Paolo Veneziano, Blaž Jurjev Trogiranin and many others. The cabinets exhibit a rich collection of silver objects from the seventeenth and the eighteenth century, tools for making lace (which made the Benedictine order famous), church clothes, as well as many manuscripts written in Croatian and books.

The church of St. Rocco was built in 1527 on the Dominican property, touching the town walls. The main altar dedicated to St. Rocco, Virgin Mary and St. Sebastian was completed during the time of Bishop Toma Speraindio. There used to be two altars next to it, one of them was dedicated to St. Justina and the other to St. Eustahius. In the nineteenth century the church was used as a mortuary and was torn down

The Kairos collection exhibits a relief of God Kairos, a deity of happy moments, made in the period between the fourth and third century BC. It was found in 1928 in the attic

in 1866. It was located in the area near the present day elementary school.

The Church of the Holy Spirit (crkva sv. Duha) was also leaning against the town walls. It is not known when the old church was built, but there is proof that in the eighteenth century a new one was built in its place. It was known for the three reliefs on its main altar. One of the oldest Trogir fraternities, Fraternity of the Holy Spirit (bratovština sv. Duha), is associated with this church. Its members even came from the ranks of nobility. The church later served as a shelter for the poor and a hospital, and was torn down in the late 1800s after being damaged in the fire.

Churches in the Center of the Old Town

The church of St. Peter once belonged to a Benedictine monastery for women. It was

Statue of St Peter, 17th C, Church of St Peter *Statue of St Paul, 17th C, Church of St Peter*

Church of St Peter – portal

designated only for the daughters of noble families and was in use until the eighteenth century. The tradition has it that the monastery was founded by Margarita, the wife of Bella the Fourth. Remains of the monastery's cloister include the courtyard with a well whose cover bears the shield of the Marković family. The Marković sisters paid for the Baroque organ case and one of the altar reliefs

Nicola Dente, bas-relief with the image of Our Lady and Blessed Augustin Kažotić, his sister Bitkula, donor next to his feet and Mary Magdalene, 14th C – lunette of the portal of the church of St Dominic

made by artist Antonio Molnari (seventeenth century). The other altar relief was made by Gregorio Lazzarini (eighteenth century). Bishop Didak Manola consecrated the church after its renovation in 1759. It has a Baroque interior, and its main altar is decorated with wooden statues of Sts. Peter and Paul. It has a decorated wooden roof restored in the early 1900s thanks to the efforts of canon priest Tacconio. Above the main entrance stands the statue of St. Peter by Nikola Firentinac.

Churches in the Town

The church and the monastery of St. Dominic are still being used by the Dominicans. The monastery was founded in 1265 on the land of Nikola Albertini. The church was constructed in the early 1300s and the Gothic cloister in the following century. The church has one nave, a bell tower and an interesting wooden ceiling with planks arranged in a shape resembling the bottom of a ship. The main entrance is on the Western side. It is decorated with a relief portraying the Virgin Mary in the middle, Blessed Augustin Kažotić on one side (figures of the donors are next to his feet) and St. Mary Magdalene on the other side. The work was made by Nicola Dente. A peculiar detail of this church is the tomb of the Sobota family found along the southern side of the Church. It was built in 1479 by the order from Katarina Sobota (known as mullerium miserrima or the most miserable woman) after horrible deaths of her son and husband which put an end to their noble family lineage. This Renaissance monument was

⇦ *View to the Monastery and Church of St Dominic*

Courtyard of the Monastery of St Dominic, ⇨
15th C

Nikola Firentinac, Vault of the Sobota Family, 15th C, church of St Dominic

built by Nikola Firentinac. The lunetta depicts the sad scene of the Mourning of Christ, and underneath it stands the coat of arms of the Sobota family and the year when it was constructed. At the bottom stands a sarcophagus with carvings of cherubs, which is being held by sculptures of two lions growling for revenge. The church's interior is decorated with paintings of the life of saints. The three most valuable are: the seventeenth century painting by Palma the Younger inside the wooden, gold plated altar, the sixteenth century paining by Jacop Constantini on the wooden retable (a raised shelf behind the altar) and the seventeenth century work by Giovanni Battiste Argeni above the altar of Our Lady of Rosary. The cloister was damaged in the British shelling during the Second World War. It was renovated after the war and the stone remains of the church of St. John the Baptist were moved to its court yard (they are nowadays located in the Museum's lapidary). One of the neighboring rooms holds an exhibit of the monastery's valuables from the 1980s. A few especially valuable pieces include: a fifteenth century polyptych sculpture of Mary With Christ made by Blaž Jurjev Trogiranin, medallion-shaped pin, and the fifteenth century Gothic reliquary from the church of the Holy Cross on Čiovo made by Trogirian goldsmiths.

The Church of All Saints is of simple build and was restored in 1598. It had two altars transferred there from the church of St. Juraj on Travarica which was destroyed in the Candian war. The seventeenth century painting by Baldassaro d'Anna hangs above the altar. In 1885 the church was closed down because if its deteriorating shape. Towards the end of 1900s the church was restored and today holds a small, private gallery bearing the same name.

The Church of Our Lady of Carmel, formerly called the Church of the New Town, used to be small and narrow. It was mentioned in the thirteenth century during the time of Šubić. In 1600s duke Dominik Minio gave a permit for its expansion. The fraternity bearing the same name, with the help of Bishop Antun Guido, funded the enlargement of the church in the early seventeenth century. Above the entrance stands the sarcophagus lid from 1348 with a figure of the crucified Christ in its middle and scenes of Annunciation in the corners. The church has a late Baroque wooden and gold plated altar with a scene of the Virgin with Christ dating back to the sixteenth century. Above the main altar hangs the seventeenth century painting of Our Lady of Carmel by Constantine Zane. During the fraternity presidency of canon priest Rikardo Tacconi in the late nineteenth century, a new fraternity house was built. Both the outside and inside of the church was renovated and a small square was rebuilt. Since the fraternity was managing the church property, enough money was saved up to purchase a bronze bust made by Špiro Kararo. It is displayed in the newly renovated sacristy.

The church of St. Mihovil stands in the Western part of Pasik. It was built as a plain looking

Palma the Younger, Circumcision of Christ, 16th C, church of St Dominic

Golden medallion with a miniature in the middle, Collection of Artefacts in the monastery of St Dominic

A Trogir square today ⇨

Loggia – interior, Nikola Firentinac, a bas-relief depicting justice, 15th C

building with a self standing bell tower. It was constructed by a fraternity on the foundations of an older church. A Benedictine monastery for middle class women, was built next to it in 1595. The church held two altars of the Gracio and Marislavić families and many paintings which came from destroyed churches. Its roof, ceilings and walls were renovated in the mid nineteenth century. During the Second World War the church was damaged by British shelling when, instead of hitting the German war ship, British planes hit the Western part of Pasik. After the war, the bell tower was restored to its original sixteenth century form.

Villas, Houses and Public Buildings

Villa Lucić is located on the waterfront and is a part of a complex of villas that were once leaning against the town walls. During the sixteenth century the grandfather of famous Ivan Lucić renovated the building in Renaissance style. Since 1850 it has been a property of family Demicheli whose redecoration and renovation destroyed the villa's original look. The main Renaissance door on the northern side remain preserved, as well as the court with arches, balconies and parts of walls. An interesting detail is a terrace on the first floor, surrounded on all four sides by villa walls.

The terrace has a well in the center, carved stone bench as well as reliefs and coat of arms on the walls. Today, the villa holds the Town Library, Study Hall, and offices of many organizations.

Villa Andreis is located in the vicinity of church of St. Peter and was built during the thirteenth century. Its main gate with a semicircular lunetta and the Andreis coat ship of arms exemplify the Romanesque style. In the fifteenth century the ground floor was redecorated in Gothic style, with two floors whose windows have pointy arches. Remains of a Gothic fireplace with double columns are found inside the villa. The building went through many ownerships, and was often redecorated. Nowadays, its is unfortunately a ruin.

Villa Cipiko is definitely one of the most beautiful preserved villas in Trogir that were created by connecting old Romanesque buildings. The villa consists of a small and large building, that were once linked by a bridge. In the fifteenth century they were redecorated by a humanist warrior Koriolan Cipiko. The building façade is decorated in gothic triforas made by Andrija Aleši. Its gate was carved by Ivan Duknović. The portal (which is now on exhibit in the Museum of the Town of Trogir) also made by Duknović depicts an angel holding a torch and the family's coat of arms. The court yard has a well, arched columns, and its southern portal was made by Nikola Firentinac. Above the door there is a decoration of angels holding a tablet which says *Nosce te ipsum* (meaning get to know yourself). The small building has a court yard with an outside stairwell and gates made by Nikola Firentinac. Next to them is a relief, allegedly made by the same artist, portraying Alvizo Cipiko. Alvizo Cipiko was the commander of the Trogirian galley bearing the name of *Zena* (woman) which took part in the Lepan battle of 1571. A legend has it that he captured and sunk the Turkish ship *Pijetao*

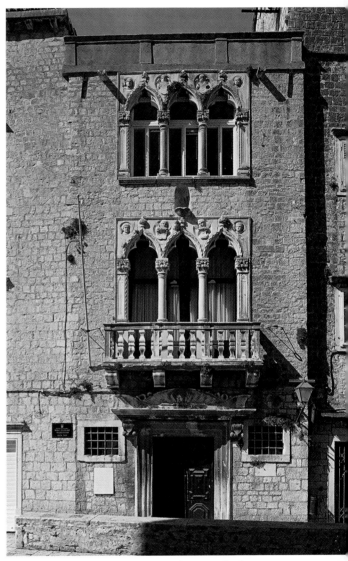

Façade of the Big Cipiko Palace – Gothic triforia, work of Andrija Aleši, portal of Ivan Duknović, 15th C

(Rooster) commanded by Captain Ali. He brought back to Trogir a sculpture of a hand holding a rooster, as his war trophy, and exhibited it in the atrium of his palace. Nowadays, a reproduction stands in its spot, while the original can be bound in the Museum of the Town of Trogir. Today, the villa is a home to the Music school, the Town's

Town Hall renovated in the Renaissance style in the 19th C

Band, Town Public Services office and a part of it is privately owned.

Villa Garangin became the home of the Museum of the Town of Trogir. The complex of villas which used to belong to the Garangin family (called Garangin-Fanfogna since 1840) consists of a few sections. The older section that went thorough many revisions over centuries, bears many looks, from the Romanesque to Baroque. The Lipavić family coats of arms are carved in the triforium peeking underneath the roof. They are works resembling Juraj Dalmatinac's style. Construction of the new section of the villa started with Baroque style in 1763 on foundations of older houses. The main entrance consists of gates with a curved arch bearing the Garangin coat of arms and two folding doors. The kitchen was located on the attic floor, and the first floor had glamorous salons (known as potrike), chapel, dining room and bedrooms. The ground floor consisted of storage rooms and basements. Commercial buildings were located in the courtyard yard, whose original floor remained preserved. In the same area stood a small Romanesque one floor building used for performing various chores and another tower-shaped building. Master Ignacije Macanović worked on the design and construction of this complex of villas.

The Museum was founded in 1963 and opened to the public in 1966. It holds collections from the following periods: Antiquity, Middle Ages (tenth to fifteenth century), salon (sixteenth to eighteenth century), and the nineteenth century, as well as an ethnographic collection. The Garagnin Fanfogna Library boasting 5581 works is one of rare completely preserved libraries. It was founded in the eighteenth century and consists of two rooms with decorated ceilings and nineteenth century cabinets. The Trogir *apendikula* (agreement between Croatian nobility and the Hungarian rulers – *Pacta conventa*) which used to belong to the library was sold in the early 1900s by the Garagnin family, struggling at the time, to the Hungarians. The Cate Dujšin Ribar Gallery opened in 1978 and exhibits works by Croatian artist Cate Dujšin Ribar who left her art work to her home town. Her artistic expression included portraits and landscapes, as well as poetry.

The lapidary opened to the public in 1987. The stone exhibition pieces are chronologically arranged from the Antiquity to Baroque period. Archeological excavations also contributed to the collection, discovering pieces such as an exposed late Antiquity tomb, remains of Hellenic and medieval buildings. The base on which each piece is exhibited is color cod-

Salon of the noble family Garagnin, 18th C, Trogir Town Museum

Library Garagnin-Fanfogna, 19th C, Trogir Town Museum

Cock, "polena" on a Turkish galley from the Battle of Lepanto in 1571 made of painted wood, Trogir Town Museum

nineteenth brought back its Renaissance look. The internal court yard exhibits the Gothic style, has a well and a stairs believed to be the work of Matej Gojković. From the seventeenth to nineteenth century a section of the first floor was used as the town theatre. Resembling the Hvar theatre, it had a ground level and box seats used by nobility and decorated with the respective family's coat of arms. The ground floor was used as a prison. The theatre was torn down at the end of the nineteenth century since it presented a fire hazard. The Town Hall was then renovated according to the blueprints made by Slado Šilović and Ante Bezić. The noble families' coats of arms were carved into the walls and remains of ruined buildings were incorporated into the Town Hall. A plaque testifying of the 1890 renovation was put on the façade. In 1935, on the 100th anniversary of the Croatian national anthem, another plaque was put next to it. In 1997 a third plaque was added, commemorating the Trogir's addition to the list of UNESCO's World Heritage sites.

The Town Loža was mentioned as early as 1311, and was once used for holding court hearings. Its present day look dates to the Renaissance period when it was renovated. The building has a shape of an arcade with two side columns, decorated with capitals from the Antiquity and Medieval periods. It was used for holding court hearings for men, while women were tried in the neighboring church of St. Mary (noble women in private residencies). Next to the clock tower stood the pillar of shame, traditionally used for serving of sentences. Its wooden part rotted away, but its chains remained. Nikola Firentinac made the relief of Justice portraying a blind folded woman sitting on a globe and holding a scale. On one of her sides stands the town protector Blessed Ivan, holding a model of Trogir in his hand. On the other side is the figure of St. Lovro and burning candles (chandelier). The judge's desk, dating

ed, so it is easy to follow which piece belongs to which period. Sculptures by artists whose work marked the period of Medieval Trogir, such as Ivan Duknović, Andrija Aleši and Nikola Firentinac are also exhibited here.

The Town Hall located in the Communal Palace, formerly the Prince's court, is a place where the prince used to live and work. Today, it serves as the mayor's office, meaning its functional purpose remained unchanged. The Town Hall building has been mentioned as early as the thirteenth century and restoration in the

Jacopo Piccino, Blessed Ivan Trogirski, Trogir Town Museum

the writing on the house of Kalebota, one of the first palm trees was planted in 1730. The French were pioneers in planting trees in the surrounding areas. In the second half of the nineteenth century Žudika and Fortin parks were put in the location of ruined walls, almost totally destroyed in the early nineteenth century. A monument to the Austrian Frank Joseph the First made by sculptor Rosandić, was put up in the Žudika park in 1910, but was torn down eight years later. Planting of trees on the island of Čiovo began in 1820 due to the efforts of general Josip Nutrizio. During his time endemic pine trees called *cempresi* were planted on the Trogir cemetery.

Until the end of the nineteenth century, people who passed away were buried in the town. During the Antiquity, they were buried on the main land section of town, and in the Medieval period in the city center. Most churches and surrounding space were used for this purpose. The honored individuals had a special place in the cathedral. The area in front of the cathedral is to this day called cimatorij. From 1814 to 1831 the cemetery was located around the church of Our Lady of Angels (crkva Gospe od Anđela) on the main land part of town where the Franciscan monastery once stood. The new cemetery and the church of Our Lady of Health (crkva Gospe od Zdravlja) were completed in 1831 in the area called Žulijan.

At the end of the eighteenth century the Garagnin family ordered a garden to be planted in the vicinity of the Dobrić spring. This garden eventually became the town park. The park consisted of smaller buildings designed by Giannantinio Selva. The horse stable was located near the road, and a vacation house called *casino* stood next to the eastern wall. Ivan Luka Garagnin had the garden decorated as a small lapidary, whose stones were brought mostly from Salona. He was one of the researchers of Salona

back to 1606, stands in front of the relief. The roof was renovated during the nineteenth century according to the design of Viennese architect Hauser. The relief portraying the Croatian ban and bishop Petar Berislavić, made by sculptor Ivan Meštrović, was placed on the southern wall.

Town Parks and Parks in the Vicinity

Care and preservation of town parks began only in the nineteenth century. Some of the larger town villas and of course monasteries had internal court yards with plants and flowers. According to

ruins as well as one of the first nominated conservators in Dalmatia. The swampy Soline area, located in the main land part of the town, was a place where salt mills once stood.

Approximately three kilometers (1.5 miles) East of the town, stands a lake. This area known as Pantan got its name from the Latin word for mud – *paulus*. The lake is rich in wet land plants and birds. Mlinice, the area where a water mill used to be is also in the vicinity – it was appropriately named the Cathedral of Bread by poet Kruno Quien. The complex consists of a long rectangular shaped building with a one floor fort in its middle which was used for defense. The rest of it was used for grinding flower. The mill was described in the legend of Golden Heart (recorded by Ante Ivančić). The water that turns the mill wheel runs from the underground spring that comes out of the Mountain of Krban. Mlinica was first mentioned in 1239 during the rule of prince Stjepko of Brbir. It was renovated on numerous occasions during the time of the Venetian rule. In the Second World War the complex was damaged in fire and is presently privately owned. After its reconstruction it will be used for tourism.

Trogir by night

Trogir – a panoramic view

THE ISLANDS

The territory of Trogir claims the islands of Čiovo, Veliki Drvenik and Mali Drvenik, all of which are inhabited, but many small uninhabited islands are also a part of the Trogir's territory.

Čiovo is the largest island, connected to the town via a draw bridge. The island is shared by Split, Trogir and Okrug. It was inhabited in the prehistoric times, and ancient Romans called it Boa (also Bua and Bavo). During the fifteenth and sixteenth century it provided refuge for the people fleeing the Turkish invasions. The south side of the island is mostly uninhabited.

The church of Our Lady of Prizidnica (crkva Gospe od Prizidnica) with hermit dwellings was built in 1546. It is located among the cliffs on the south side of the island. The village of Slatine on the side facing Split was most likely inhabited prior to the Middle Ages. In the fifteenth and sixteenth century population of the village increased. There used to be an Old Croatian church of St. Peter (crkva sv. Petra) in the bay of Supetarska. In the middle ages the church of St. Margaret (crkva sv. Mare), whose remains are still visible, was built next to it. The Church of Ascension of Mary (crkva

Trogir islets – Veliki Drvenik

Marijina Uznesenja) was built in the seventeenth century and was enlarged two centuries later.

The village of Žedno is located in the island's center and has the church of St. Mauro (crkva sv. Mavra). The church stands on a field where hermits used to gather. In the village center is the church of the Blessed Ivan the Trogirian (crkva bl. Ivana Trogirskog). Arbanija is a village by the sea whose Dominican monastery of St. Cross (sv. Križa) was founded in the fifteenth century. The monastery complex has a cloister with a spacious garden. It is interesting to note that the monastery's northern wall was built as a protective and defensive fort. The church holds a valuable collection of paintings. It includes works by Matej Ponzonio Poncun from the seventeenth century, Agostin Pitteri from the

eighteenth century and Antonio Molinaro from the seventeenth century.

In the village of Čiovo, above the cave where hermits once used to live, stands the Franciscan monastery of St. Anthony (sv. Ante). It still looks the same as it did back in the seventeenth century. The monastery has the gold plated silver crown decorated with jewels and dating back to the 1300's. It also keeps the statue of St. Magdalene made by Ivan Duknović and many paintings, the most famous painted by Jacopo Palmo the Younger from the seventeenth century. The church of St. Lazarus (crkva sv. Lazara) from the 1400's used to be an integral part of the monastery. During the time of the plague, those who were infected resided in poor people's houses located next to the monastery. In the early 1800's this complex

Franciscan Monastery and the church of St Anthony on the islet of Čiovo

Crown of gilt silver adorned with jewels, 14th C, Franciscan monastery of St Anthony

was made into a school. Today, the church is called St. Joseph's (crkva sv. Josipa) and keeps the painting by Matej Ponzonio Pončun from the sixteenth/seventeenth century. The medieval church of St. Jacob (sv. Jakova) later acquired the Baroque look. It has works of art whose authors are not known. Smaller churches on the island of Čiovo include St. Nicholas' (fourteenth century) and St. Andreas' (sixth/seventh century). The church of Our Lady by the Sea (crkva Gospe pokraj mora) belongs to the early Romanesque style and is decorated with Renaissance details. It was built in memory of the victory over the people of Split. According to the legend it was a site where Bishop Berislavić held his first mass.

Okrug (also known as Okruk) Gornji and Okrug Donji make up a separate township nowadays, but used to be a part of Trogir. They have St. Tudor's (crkva sv. Tudora) and St. Carl Boromeian (crkva sv. Karla Boromejskog) churches.

The islands of Veliki Drvenik and Mali Drvenik hold remains of Roman villas, the so called villa rustica (Roman Tariona). In the early 1400's the islands were inhabited by new peoples who arrived from the Viniški area on the mainland. The parish church of St. George (sv. Juraj) is located on Drvenik Veliki and was built in the sixteenth century. It has a Gothic altar which was designed by Master Ignacij Macanović during its renovation in the eighteenth century. The church has two eighteenth century paintings by Antonio Grapinelli. The village also has a summer home of the Moretti family as well as late Baroque residential and defensive complexes decorated with remains of Antiquity and Romanesque structures.

Jacopo Palma the Younger, St Anthony ⇨ the Abbot and St Paul the hermit, Franciscan Monastery of St Anthony on Čiovo

Islet of Čiovo

THE VICINITY OF TROGIR

The vicinity of Trogir nowadays includes two townships, Seget and Marina, both of which used to be an integral part of the Trogir territory. The main sources of income for their population used to be fishing and farming, but nowadays people earn their income mostly from tourism. Seget has many large hotel complexes and campsites.

Seget Gornji is located in the inland, while Seget Donji was build on the coast. The former exemplifies a type of perfectly enclosed settlement. It was founded in 1564 when a Trogirian nobleman Jakov Rotondo received a permit to build a fortress, around which a town developed. Until 1750 there used to be a small church of Our Lady of Rosary and St. Anton Padovian standing on the town's main square. After this old church was torn down, a new one was built in its place in 1758.

The Segetsko field has many ancient churches. Remains of the church of St. Daniel (Sudanel) most likely dates back to the Preromanesque period. The church of St. Vid, dating back to the twelfth or thirteenth century and renovated in the seventeenth century is very small and has a belfry. Remains of the fourteenth century church of St. Mihovil are located in the area known as

Seget Donji

Lavdir. The name of Zemlja Sv. Nikole (The land of St.Nicholas) carries the same name as the fourteenth century church. The fourteenth century Our Lady of Snow (Gospa od Zvirača) was built in Romanesque and Gothic styles. Our Lady of Konacvina (Gospa od Konacvina) is a tomb chapel decorated in many different styles, from Gothic to the Renaissance. The church of St. Ilija of Thunder (St. Ilija Gromovnik) was built on a hill in the thirteenth century.

Marina, which according to old pieces of literature used to be called Bosiljina, was first mentioned in written documents in 1200 as a village whose earnings were collected by the Trogirian dukes and the Church. In 1495, Bishop Franjo Marcel was granted a permit from the Trogirian duke Alviz Barbariga to build a tower in the Marina bay. The tower was to have a defensive purpose, and soon enough a village was formed around it. During the same time, the bishop built the church of St. Marina. This Renaissance church dedicated to St John the Baptist (crkva sv. Ivana Krstitelja) whose belfry, received its church clock from Trogir in 1866. It exhibits Preromanesque remains of altar architrave which were found during the restoration work inside the church and around it. The parish church of St. Jacob (crkva sv. Jakova) dates back to the eighteenth century. The church has many eighteenth and nineteenth century works of art whose authors are unknown. The chapel inside the cave of St. Jacob and Filip (sv. Jakov i Filip) has a painting made by an unknown author from the

Marina

Vinišća

Old mills near Trogir – Pantan

seventeenth century. Remains of ancient fortresses can be found on the Drid hill near Marina. This area was inhabited in the prehistoric times, most likely because of its strategic importance. Nowadays, the church of St. Mary of Drid (crkva sv. Marije od Drida) stands on the hill. When the area was

evacuated in fear of Turkish invasions, the church's pieces of ecclesiastical adoration and the painting of Our lady of Drid was taken to the Franciscan monastery on Čiovo.

The neighboring village of Vinišće was mentioned in the 1272 documents of the Trogir bishopric. However, the exact founding date of this settlement has not been determined. Judging by the Illyrian structures and remains of the Roman civilization, this area must have been inhabited prior to the medieval ages. During the Middle ages the area was divided into two parts: Biskupija, the coastal region and Opatija, the inland region where the village of Orihovica is located. Orihovica is the home of the Duknović family to which belongs sculptor Ivan Duknović.

Turkish invasions caused many families to escape to the neighboring islands and it was not until the eighteenth century that the people started immigrating to the area.

The church of the Blessed Virgin Mary (also known as the church of St. Juraj) in Orihovica was founded by the Benedictine monks in 1272. The church was surrounded by a cemetery with tombstones known as stećci. The church of St. Anton Padovian (also known as Our Lady of Carmel) was built in the eighteenth century in the center of the village of Vinišće. The new parish church of the Heart of Jesus holds a nineteenth century paining whose author is unknown.

The Church of St. John on the cape of Ploča was built in 1332. The legend has it that it was erected in the spot where the Blessed John Trogirian miraculously saved some shipwrecked people from Šibenik.

The inland villages of Ljubovitica, Prapatnica, Bristvica, Blizna, Mitlo and Vinovac each have their own church dedicated to their respective patron saint. The oldest one for sure is the church of St. Mary in Blizna which dates back to the ninth century.

ENTERTAINMENT

The town center of Trogir has many nice coffee shops and cafes, pleasant restaurants and small, privately run hotels. During the Summer there are many classical music and rock concerts taking place, as well as performances of visiting theatre groups. There is an open roof movie theatre and performances of local groups, such as People's Band, KUD (Cultural and Arts Group) Kvadria which performs traditional folklore dances, the Petar Berislavić quire, children quire Cimblići, etc. Some cafes will have their own entertainment. The discotheque is located near the town, and for young people who like to dance, the discotheque in Primošten is also close by. During the summer, the Museum of the Town of Trogir holds various types of exhibitions. Visitors can sightsee the town's monuments, museums, churches, galleries and souvenir shops. The street booths sell many souvenirs which will always remind one of the unforgettable visit to Trogir.

Trogir "cakavci" in the square

The neighboring county of Seget has larger hotel complexes, such as the tourist resort Medena which consists of both hotels and apartments. Medena has recreational and tourist facilities such as: tennis and basketball courts, fitness room, night bars, an enclosed swimming pool, a private beech, and many water activities. The marina has a small hotel and private accommodation, which is also available in the country of Okrug. The so called ribarske večeri (fisherman nights) are famous celebrations everywhere and include fish and wine tasting, performances of traditional vocal bands called klape, etc.

The winters are naturally much less exciting. However, even during this period there are exhibitions, lectures, book presentations, music school concerts etc, which appeals to those who like a peaceful vacation.

All of these things make the area an attractive tourist destination throughout the year.

"Trabakuli" in the port

Beaches, islets

"Medena"Hotel – Seget Donji

CONTENTS

Quay in the night